Demos is an independent think tank committed to radical thinking on the long-term problems facing the UK and other advanced industrial societies.

It aims to develop ideas – both theoretical and practical – to help shape the politics of the twenty first century, and to improve the breadth and quality of political debate.

Demos publishes books and a regular journal and undertakes substantial empirical and policy oriented research projects. Demos is a registered charity.

In all its work Demos brings together people from a wide range of backgrounds in business, academia, government, the voluntary sector and the media to share and cross-fertilise ideas and experiences.

For further information and
subscription details please contact:
Demos
Panton House
25 Haymarket
London SW1Y 4EN
email: mail@demos.co.uk
www.demos.co.uk

Other publications available from Demos:

The Common Sense of Community
The Return of the Local
To Our Mutual Advantage
Tomorrow's Politics

To order a publication or
a free catalogue please contact Demos.

The Third Way to a Good Society

Amitai Etzioni

DEM◉S

First published in 2000 by
Demos
Panton House
25 Haymarket
London SW1Y 4EN

ISBN 1 84180 030 9
Printed in Great Britain by Redwood Books
Design by Lindsay Nash

Contents

Acknowledgements

This document grew out of a discussion between Geoff Mulgan and myself. I am indebted to Tom Bentley for numerous and detailed suggestions and queries. I also benefitted greatly form comments by Steven Lukes, John Gray, Martin Albrow and Robin Niblett for comments on a previous draft. The book was helped much by editorial assistance by Natalie Klein, Jennifer Ambrosino, and Rachel Mears and from Matthew Horne and Jason Marsh for research assistance.

A rather different version of this book will be published in the United States under the title *Next: on the way to the good society*, by Basic Books.

Foreword

The 'Third Way' debate has, so far, been a failure. The shaping of a distinctive philosophy which can inform the policy and practice of a new centre-left remains in its early stages. This is ironic, given the worldwide level of energy and commitment being poured into the search for a new political synthesis.

However, it is not surprising given the complexity of the task. Those engaged in it are grappling with an external environment which many still struggle to understand. The scale and complexity of economic, social, technological and environmental change are unprecedented. Simple ideological formulas do not provide policy solutions or command widespread electoral support. Citizens are increasingly sceptical, and politicians must contend both with higher levels of expectations and with widespread disengagement from the whole of formal politics.

There is also serious confusion over the nature of the project itself. Is the Third Way an abstract philosophy, an approach to political leadership and management, or a distinctive set of policies? Should it be all three? The weak connections between these three missions are one explanation for the failure so far. For those seeking further renewal in specific areas such as health, education or neighbourhood regeneration, the absence of a big picture frustrates their attempts to build a coherent, long-term strategy. The politics of the age, dominated as they are by media management, personality and pragmatism, often seem at odds with the call for a long-term, ethical approach to politics and public life.

These factors often obscure the debate in all systems, but in the UK they are especially pronounced. Despite the power, energy and initial popularity of New Labour, it has suffered from a key weakness: the inability to root its policies and pronouncements deeply in a surrounding context. New Labour has only taken concrete shape since Tony Blair's election as party leader in 1994, and its nature has been oppositional – not only was the 1997 election won through effective critique of the incumbent government, but many of New Labour's symbolic acts, such as rewriting of Clause Four, were calculated to distance the party from its own history. These facts mean that the Third Way, as an experiment in government, has had shallow roots.

As a result, the UK government has been open to several criticisms, despite its success in stimulating debate. The first is that it is excessively pragmatic, using the 'what works' slogan to choose its policy interventions without recourse to a coherent overall framework; the Third Way in practice has sometimes looked like 'what we are doing this week'. The second is that the gap between rhetoric and reality has been too wide: Blair's promise of a new politics and a new kind of society have masked a set of changes which are largely seen as incremental, and made possible only by a sustained period of economic growth which will not last.

But there are other, deeper reasons for the failure of this debate. One reason is the relationship between theory, or ideology, and practice. The discussion and formation of political theory has become a specialist activity, restricted largely to universities, some sections of the media and a narrow group of other elites. Those who produce big ideas are often not responsible for understanding how to implement them. Yet innovation in practice has become a definitive test of the new politics. Theory is not enough if it does not inform an approach to organisational life – whether it be the governance of communities, the delivery of healthcare or conduct of education. Governments are trying to adapt to an environment in which they effect change not so much through large-scale macro-decision making, but through sustained campaigns of persuasion and cultural change.

In this context, where organisations must innovate radically in order to survive, many theorists have been severely challenged by the need to engage with concrete issues of policy and practise. Their theories and bit ideas do not convert easily into policy-makers' strategy. Nor does their work inspire or inform dedicated practitioners.

Another underlying reason is the inadequacy of our international dialogue. Most of the domestic problems with which the government struggles – reforming welfare and education systems, generating employment, making communities safe – will only be solved if different polities are able to learn rapidly from experience in other systems. Alongside these are the problems without frontiers – immigration and refugee movements, environmental protection, and so on – which require effective international collaboration for there to be any hope of success. There are moves to strengthen and energise this international dialogue, as the recent Berlin summit on 'progressive governance' showed. Yet our capacity for debating such issues, and the political questions which underpin them, is still severely limited. Many international accounts are either so general as to be meaningless in a specific context, or so technical and detailed that they cannot be connected to broader, more ideological discussion.

In this context, Amitai Etzioni's pamphlet offers a major step forward. As the leading communitarian thinker of his age, his use of the phrase 'Third Way' preceded the existence of New Labour, and is rooted in a clear and compelling vision of the good society. At the core of the argument is the idea of the Third Way as an ethical position derived from the need to treat people as ends in themselves, rather than as instruments in the pursuits of other goals.

Etzioni argues that the good society rests on the proper balance between state, market and community. The argument itself makes clear and direct connections between theory and practice providing concrete examples of how its ethical imperative can be carried through in different spheres. He offers a definition of community which is rich enough to have meaning, but flexible enough to incorporate all kinds of community from the neighbourhood to the virtual.

Communities, he argues are indispensable in providing meaning and purpose to individual lives. But they are also a key provider of collective solutions for which others turn solely to the state or the market. This question, of how social need can be met through community-based organisations, will become increasingly important over the next decade.

The analysis points directly to major challenges for the Third Way, in particular that of limiting inequality which many politicians are currently uncomfortable in addressing. Etzioni argues that while the last vestiges of elitism and discrimination should be eradicated, such symbolic acts must be underpinned by a form of basic economic equality which may be at odds with current trends.

Perhaps the most important, in the long term, is the role he assigns to moral dialogue as a way of framing and shaping change. While shared moral culture is an integral part of the good society, in Etzioni's account such a culture is not fixed or static. Progressive change is stimulated and managed through a wide-ranging process of dialogue which can encompass whole societies, though political leaders carry particular responsibility for initiating and listening to it. His final plea, for a grand debate about the relationship between material consumption and well-being, points to one of the fundamental challenges which progressive politics faces over the next two decades.

Tom Bentley
Director, Demos
June 2000

1. The good society: first principles

The vision

We need a clearer vision of where the Third Way is taking us. While debates on improvements to public programmes or legal structures fascinate some, most people are not interested in technocratic details. They yearn for a vision of where we are headed, one that provides a way of assessing past accomplishments and plans for the future. Such a vision inspires and compels; it lends meaning to our endeavours and sacrifices, to our lives.

We aspire to a society that is not merely civil but is good. A good society is one in which people treat one another as ends in themselves and not merely as instruments; as whole persons rather than as fragments; as members of a community, bonded by ties of affection and commitment, rather than only as employees, traders, consumers or even as fellow citizens. In the terms of the philosopher Martin Buber, a good society nourishes 'I-Thou' relations, although it recognises the inevitable and significant role of 'I-It' relations.

Some core values of a good society can be directly derived from its definition. Child abuse, spousal abuse, violent crime in general and of course civil and international war offend the basic principle of treating people as ends. Hence, our love of peace. Furthermore, we hold that violating individual autonomy, unless there are strong compelling public needs, is incompatible with treating people as ends. This the ultimate foundation of our commitment to liberty.

When we find value in creating or appreciating art, music and other expressions of culture, or engage in learning for its own sake, we typically are in the realm of ends. In contrast, when we trade in these items we are in the instrumental realm, which is quite legitimate as long as it does not intrude on, let alone dominate, that of ends.

When we bond with family, friends or community members we live up to the basic principle of the good society. The values of love, loyalty, caring and community all find their roots here. In contrast, when we 'network' – bonding for a utilitarian purpose rather for its own sake – we abandon this realm.

The relationship of the basic principle to social justice is a complex one. The priority of treating people as ends requires more than equality of opportunity but less than equality of outcomes; it denotes a rich basic minimum for all. Still other values arise more indirectly, we shall see, out of moral dialogues. These seek to limit conflict and cultural wars and put a premium on reaching shared understandings – a major attribute of good societies.

The ethical tenet that people are to be treated as purposes rather than only as means is commonly recognised. Less widely accepted is the significant sociological observation that it is in communities, not in the realm of the state or the market, that this tenet is best institutionalised.

Equally pivotal is the recognition that only in a society where no one is excluded, and all are treated with equal respect, are all people accorded the status of being ends in themselves and allowed to reach their full human potential. Furthermore, the core communitarian idea – that we have inalienable individual rights *and* social responsibilities for each other – is based on the same basic principle: we are both *entitled* to be treated as ends in ourselves and are *required* to treat others and our communities in this way.

The good society is one that balances three often partially incompatible elements: the state, the market and the community. This is the underlying logic of the statements above. The good society does not seek to obliterate these segments but to keep them properly nourished – and contained.

Similarly, much has been made already of the fact that the Third Way (Neue Mitte, centrist approach, communitarian thinking) does not view the government as the problem or as the solution but as one partner of the good society. Nor it does not see the market as a source of all that is good or evil but as a powerful economic engine that must be accorded sufficient space to do its work while also guarded properly.

Different Third Way societies still struggle with finding the proper point of balance. The continental societies still have a long way to go toward curtailing the state and allowing the market to function properly. The United States may well have overshot the point of balance by according the market too much space. The UK might be drawing closer to the point of balance. However, the third partner of the good society – the community – has not been given its proper share of the social division of labour in any Third Way society.

The vision of a good society is a tableau on which we project our aspirations, not a full checklist of all that deserves our dedication. And the vision is often reformulated as the world around us changes, and as we change. Moreover, it points to different steps that different societies best undertake, depending on their place on the Third Way. But the ultimate vision is one and the same.

The good society is an ideal. While we may never quite reach it, it guides our endeavours and we measure our progress by it.

The Third Way

The Third Way is a road that leads us toward the good society. However, it should be acknowledged at the outset that the Third Way is indeed fuzzy at the edges, not fully etched. As the *Economist* wrote about the Third Way, 'Trying to pin down an exact meaning is like wrestling an inflatable man. If you get a grip on one limb, all the hot air rushes to another.'[1] Professor Steven Teles of Brandeis University has called the Third Way 'a masterwork of ambiguity'.[2] But this is one of the main virtues of this approach: it points to the directions that we ought to follow, but is neither doctrinaire nor a rigid ideological system.

The Third Way is not American, British or the property of any other nation or region or culture. Among its numerous origins are the Old and the New Testament; the teachings of the Ancient Greeks; Asian, Muslim and Jewish conceptions of harmony and responsibility for others than self; Fabian thinking; Catholic social thought; and much else.[3]

The Third Way has often been depicted in negative terms, in terms of that which it is not. It is correctly stated as neither a road paved by statist socialism nor one underpinned by the neoliberalism of the free market. It tilts neither to the right or the left. (In the US – which has had no significant socialist tradition – the Third Way runs between a New Deal conception of big state, which administers large-scale social programmes and extensively regulates the economy, and a libertarian or laissez faire unfettered market.)[4]

Here, an attempt is made to provide it with a positive and normative characterisation as a public philosophy that both provides principles and points to public policy implications. Above all, we suggest changes people will have to introduce into their own ways of conduct and their institutions.

Is there one Third Way or multiple Third Ways? While some societies drive more in the left lane (France, Italy) and some more on the right (the United States), the road they all travel is fully distinct from the one charted by totalitarian and libertarian approaches. Moreover, while the various Third Way societies differ in their specific synthesis of the ways of the state and the market, they are pulling closer to one another.

Much has been written about the need to find a way that will allow European economies to compete globally but not become Americanised; to enhance economic flexibility and productivity but not yield all to the service of mammon; to develop a new European social model. Much of what follows addresses these questions by focusing on two key issues: the role of community on the Third Way and the need to set clear limits on how far one ought to tilt in the American direction.

2. The roles of the community

The neglected partner

Communities defined

Communities are the main social entities that nourish ends-based (I-Thou) relationships, while the market is the realm of means-based (I-It) relationships. The state–citizen relationship also tends to the instrumental. While some people bond at work and some barter in communities, by and large without communities a deficit in ends-based relationships is sure to be pronounced. As John Gray put it, 'the flourishing of individuals presupposes strong and deep forms of common life.'[5] In short, communities are a major component of good societies.

The concept of community is often said to be vague and ellusive. This charge is also made against other widely used concepts such as class, elites and even rationality. Communities, in my understanding, are based on two foundations, both of which reinforce I-Thou relationships. First, communities provide bonds of affection that turn groups of people into social entities resembling extended families. Second, they transmit a shared moral culture (a set of shared social meanings and values that characterise what the community considers virtuous versus unacceptable behaviour) from generation to generation, as well as reformulating this moral framework day by day. These traits differentiate communities from other social groups.

While in earlier eras, and to some extent today, communities were largely residential (membership was geographically defined, as in villages), this is now often not the case. Contemporary communities evolve among members of one profession working for the same institution (for example, the physicians of a given hospital or the faculty of a college); members of an ethnic or racial group even if dispersed among others (a Jewish community or one of Bangladeshi immigrants in east London); people who share a sexual orientation; or intellectuals of the same political or cultural feather. Some communities are quite large, and in part imagined; for instance, many gay men visiting another part of the country know socially some people who live there and feel close to others they meet there for the first time.

Groups that merely share a specific interest – to prevent the internet from being taxed or to reduce the costs of postage – are solely an interest group or lobby. They lack the affective bonds and shared culture that make communities into places that truly involve people rather than focusing on a narrow facet of their lives.

Critics correctly point out that communities are not necessarily places of brotherly and sisterly love; they may be oppressive, intolerant, nasty. This is largely true of communities in earlier eras. In democratic societies, people often choose which communities to join and participate in, making communities as a rule less overpowering. While even contemporary communities are far from perfect, the same obviously holds for the state and the market. We must stop comparing existing social entities to some visionary utopia and ask instead how they can be improved. And we must recognise that each of the three partners is better (not necessarily good) at some tasks than the others. Communities are often overlooked as a very important social factor even by Third Way advocates, who tend to focus on seeking the proper balance between the state and the market.[6] In a well-balanced society all three complement and contain one another.

The relative advantage of communities

The special capacity of communities to move us toward the good society is highlighted by the finding that people who live in communities live longer, healthier and more content lives than people who are bereft of such membership. They are likely to have significantly fewer psychosomatic illnesses and mental health problems than those who live in isolation. And, with their craving for sociality well sated, community members are much less likely to join violent gangs, religious cults or militias.

The fact that social isolation is dangerous for mental health was high-lighted in 1955 during the first mission to establish a US base in Antarctica, where isolation provoked paranoid psychosis.[7] Since then, numerous studies have shown that isolation significantly increases various psychological health risks.[8] In their classic study of New Yorkers lonely in high-rise apartments, *Mental Health in the Metropolis*, Leo Srole and his associates found that 60 per cent of the residents had sub-clinical psychiatric conditions and 20 per cent were judged psychologically impaired.[9] Numerous studies have demonstrated that, after work-related stress, the most important social factor in mental health is marital, familial and friendship relationships.[10]

A study published in *The Lancet* medical journal found that elderly people who live alone, have no friends or have a bad relationship with their children were 60 per cent more likely to develop dementia than those whose social contacts were more satisfying. The more socially isolated elderly people were, the more likely they were to develop the brain condition.[11]

Communities, data shows, can play a major role in providing preventive and acute care, reducing the need for publicly funded social services as divergent as childcare, grief counselling and professional drug and alcohol abuse treatment, as well as assisting in curtailing juvenile delinquency.

The strongest evidence for these statements is found in religious communities that meet my definition of shared affective bonds and a moral culture. Practically all kinds of anti-social behaviour are relatively low among Mormon communities in Utah, Orthodox Jewish communities in New York and Black Muslim groups. They are also lower on average in villages and small town America as compared to large cities, in which communities are often weaker.

There are scores of studies similar to the ones summarised here that highlight communities' important role. Patrols of volunteers, called Orange Hats, chased drug dealers out of their neighborhood in Washington DC. In the process, members of the community also became closer to one another.

In 1988, Wellsburg, West Virginia had a particularly high incidence of heart disease – 29 per cent above the national average. By 1996, the community's cardiovascular health profile was among the best in the state, according to a study conducted by Mary Lou Hurley and Lisa Schiff.[12] The improvement reflected community organised walks, healthy potluck suppers and numerous classes in aerobics and ways to reduce cholesterol, blood pressure and stress. A screening of 182 community members found that they had maintained their weight loss and most of the reduction in cholesterol and blood pressure.[13] According to the researchers, 'the average wellness score ... topped the 1988 baseline by 12 per cent and the average fitness score by 42 per cent.'[14]

In the county of Tillamook, Oregon, diverse community groups, including religious and liberal ones, decided to collaborate on the problem of teenage pregnancy, leading to a decrease from 24 pregnancies per 1,000 girls age ten to seventeen in 1990 to seven per 1,000 in 1994.[15]

These are but a few illustrative findings. Aside from significantly reducing public costs, communal provisions such as these are often much more individually tailored than public programmes and can be made much less alienating than government action.

Ergo, next
For all these reasons, cultivating communities where they exist, and helping them form where they have been lost, is essential for future provision of much social good; it should be a major priority for future progress along the Third Way.

In the next decade communities should be increasingly relied upon to shoulder a greater share of our social missions, because – to reiterate – they can fulfil them at lower public costs and with greater humanity than either the state or the market. They may well be the most important new source of social services in the foreseeable future, as the ability to increase taxes to pay for social services is nearly exhausted and the total costs of social services will continue to rise at rates higher than inflation.[16]

Seeking much greater reliance on communities is not an attempt to replace the welfare state. On the contrary, by reducing the burden on the welfare state, communities help to sustain it.

Existing public policies and procedures should be reviewed regularly to ensure that the renewal and maintenance of existing communities is not inadvertently undermined (for example, by pre-empting their natural roles) and to ensure that they opportune community development on a local, regional and societal level.

To foster communities, the prime minister may call on all ministers to provide him annually with reports on steps to involve communities more in their work; community 'audits' could further assess where there is room for greater community involvement; and statistics ought to be published regularly about progress in the needed direction. However, experience shows that such measures are much more effective if they are represented, symbolically and in practice, by high-profile institutions. This strongly suggests that a special division should be created within a suitable ministry (for example, the Home Office or the Department for the Environment, Transport and the Regions) or, better yet, create a new ministry dedicated to community development. While critics are likely to complain about centralism, forming some kind of permanent taskforce for community development in a government department would further reinforce this important mission.

Much has been made in recent years about the new ways through which the state might project itself. It has been said it should be a 'enabler and a catalyst' rather than itself directing and financing social programmes. This postmodern style of management is said to be flat rather than hierarchical, based on networking rather than directive; that public goals can be serve indirectly via the market. A good part of this is true, and needs no repeating here. Some of it is over-hyped. The management style most suited for social work may not be the same for building a destroyer and so on. Above all, Third Way management styles must be tailored not merely to take into account various combinations of the state and the market but also to involve communities.

Mutuality and voluntary associations

A good society relies even more on mutuality than on voluntarism. Mutuality is a form of community relationship in which people help each other rather than merely helping those in need.[17] The Neighborhood Watch scheme and anti-crime patrols by community volunteers, such as in Balsall Heath, Birmingham, where crime was reduced by six-citizen teams regularly patrolling the streets,[18] are examples of mutuality. So are consumer and producer cooperatives, like Local Food Buying Groups and mutual saving associations such as credit unions.[19] Fostering Tenant Management Associations in council estates rather than relying mainly on government or profit-making management is another case in point.

Mutuality-based associations have always existed and have been on the rise in recent years. Still, they need to be greatly expanded, encouraged and furbished with the needed resources in order to carry more of the social burdens in the years to come.

Mutuality is commonly and naturally practiced among family members, friends, neighbours, colleagues and members of voluntary associations. It can be an important source of childcare (such as in parent cooperatives, where parents provide a few hours of service each week, thereby reducing public costs and providing natural staff accountability); sick care (for instance, when people are discharged 'early' from hospitals to be helped by kin and other community members); grief support; and much else.

Mutual help groups (oddly often called self-help groups) can play a major role coping with cancer, contagious diseases, alcoholism, obesity and the like (probably the best known is the highly successful Alcoholics Anonymous).[20] They are a vastly underused resource. In the new century, public services, especially the National Health Service and welfare agencies, should greatly increase efforts highlighting the value of such groups, as well as help prime them and provide resources. They must, however, ensure that their role in initiating and conducting these groups does not sap these groups' natural communal flows or stunt their development.

Mutuality is undermined when treated like an economic exchange of services. (Undermining occurs, for example, when governments pay friends to be friends as some countries do to ensure that someone visits and informally assists those discharged from hospitals.) Mutuality is based on an open-ended moral commitment. In mutual relationships, people do not keep books on each other but have a generalised expectation that the other will do his or her turn if and when a need arises. Public policies and arrangements that attempt to organise mutuality as if it were an exchange will tend to undermine this moral foundation. Examples of such policies are 'time banks', in which hours spent babysitting, for example, are recorded and the same amount of hours in voluntary service are expected in return, or establishing programmes like used clothing exchanges, in which the amount of clothes one contributes determines the amount one receives from the exchange. Much looser, more informal 'arrangements' – of the kind that prevail among people who 'exchange' gifts – are preferred. At the same time, posting on a website or other public place the time contributions various members of a community have made, as one does for financial donations, may help foster such contributions.

To favour mutuality is not to make light of voluntarism. Indeed, it should be further encouraged. A good start in this direction are Chancellor Gordon Brown's policies encouraging a spirit of voluntarism and civic patriotism. His measures include matching people who want to offer their time and money through voluntary work with charitable and voluntary organisations seeking volunteers, via a dedicated website.

Mr Brown's plan also calls for new incentives to encourage pay-packet donations. People will be able, through the scrapping of the £250 minimum limit for donations to attract tax relief, to give as much as they like. And they will be encouraged to make gifts of shares.

The importance of voluntarism for community building, civic spirit and democratic government has been set out many times and requires no repetition. It should be noted, however, that several Third Way societies, especially on the continent, still have a long way to go before voluntarism is properly developed and can assume its share of the social business that must be conducted.

Voluntarism is best carried out, whenever possible, in the service learning mode. *Service learning* is a form of voluntarism in which those who serve do not maintain they are acting purely through altruism but instead acknowledge that they themselves benefit educationally and socially from their experience. It is especially compatible with the ideal of treating people as ends, although all forms of voluntarism are preferable to pure means-based relationships.

The question often arises: who will be able to provide more time for mutuality and voluntarism, given that more and more women, who used to be a major source of both, are now in paid employment? One answer may well be senior citizens. They are a rapidly growing class; live longer and healthier lives than their predecessors; consume a growing proportion of the societal resources; and would greatly benefit from staying involved in pro-social roles. Without their contribution, societies may well not be able to attend to a large and growing portions of its social business.

While each member of every community ought to be both required and expected to make contributions to the common good above and beyond that of their own community (for instance, by paying taxes due in full), they should be allowed, indeed encouraged, to provide 'extras' for their own community. Hence, it is crucial for communities to be free to levy some form of fees, dues or taxes above those levied by the state. Parents should be welcomed when they contribute services, money and assets to their children's schools rather than be expected to put their resources into an anonymous pot from which all schools may draw. Ethically, it is too heroic to expect that people will be willing to do for one and all as much as they are willing to do for their own communities. And limiting contributions to universal pots is incompatible with a society that views communities as essential, constitutive social entities.

At the same time, communities should be encouraged to care about the fate of other communities; for example, better-off communities should be expected to help those less endowed. To the extent they assist their sister communities, the affluent ones could be celebrated and given tax benefits. Special levies could be dedicated to specific projects, making them more readily accepted than increases in general taxes.

Much more realistic and valuable programmes are regional ones, in which communities help one another with arrangements that could vary from a rapid transit system to coordinating police efforts, from building highway and bridges to sharing an airport. These sharing arrangements are often quite properly touted as enhancing efficiency (indeed many would not be possible without regional collaboration). However, they often – although by no means always – do serve as somewhat indirect forms of reallocation of resources, as the better-off communities pick up a larger share of the costs than the others, or the less endowed ones reap a disproportionate part of the benefits generated.

Pro-community public policies

Community renewal can be enhanced by providing occasions for social gatherings (for example, opening schools for community meetings, fostering neighborhood street festivals). Temporary organisers can be assigned to an area to initiate group formations. And community renewal benefits from improving the physical conditions, safety and accessibility of public spaces. (For a compelling example, see the discussion of schools as community hubs by Tom Bentley and by Ben Jupp.)[21]

Renewal is also fostered by inviting groups of people who share the use of a property, area or public service to participate in decision-making regarding its use. Examples include citizens setting the hours a park is open, who may use it (children *and* dogs?) and for what purposes (public assembly or communing with nature?). More support must be given to groups of citizens, like those who set park opening times and bylaws in the Phoenix Community Park near Charing Cross Road in central London.[22] Calling on such groups to assume some responsibility for maintaining shared facilities can further enhance bonds among the members. Major benefits can be achieved if people are helped to from shopping co-ops, mutual saving and loan associations, and other forms of economic organisation that parallel and hence enforce communal bonds.

For communities to flourish, public policies must take into account that often communities' boundaries do not conform to administrative ones. These boundaries should be tailored to the communities' lines rather than attempt to make communities adhere to a preset administrative geography.

In addition, public policies need to be tailored to smaller social units than are often encompassed in one administrative district, because communities are often smaller. This applies to policies such as the New Deal for Communities, aimed at smaller neighbourhoods of 2,000-5,000 people, and the National Strategy for Neighborhood Renewal. The reorganisation of core social policy programmes around smaller neighbourhood units is an ongoing priority. Increased devolution allows more citizens to participate in their own government, become more politically engaged and increase their civic skill and effect. For instance, neighborhood officers entrusted with patrolling local areas for deteriorating facilities, environmental problems and social conflicts can be helpful especially if elected rather than appointed, and if their priorities are set either solely by the affected communities or at least in close consultation with them.

Policy-makers should take into account that communities need not be residential or include members who live next to one another. Communities can form around institutions (universities, hospitals) or professions (longshoremen, accountants). They are often ethnically based and can even form in cyberspace (virtual communities). Best results are achieved when communities that already share social bonds are further reinforced by providing them with access to a shared online 'wired' space.

Thriving communities often need core institutions such as local schools, courthouses, post offices and downtown shopping areas. Under some conditions, such as when an area has been largely depopulated, it might make sense to yield to considerations of economic and administrative efficiency and consolidate or 'regionalise' such institutions or allow downtown shopping to be replaced by supermalls. However, such economic and administrative efficiencies should never be considered the only relevant considerations. To put it differently, a Third Way society gives much weight to social costs that include costs resulting from the loss of community when its core institutions are shut down. Only when non-social considerations clearly outweigh social ones should core institutions, the mainstays of community, be closed.

Community safety

Policies that seek to sustain or renew communities must take into account that communities are formed and reinforced largely in public spaces rather than in the privacy of one's home or car. To the extent that these spaces are unsafe or depleted, communities are diminished. Therefore, communities should take special care to maintain public playgrounds, sidewalks, pedestrian walkways, parks and plazas. For non-residential communities this might entail providing meeting spaces in, for instance, public schools or libraries; setting aside segments of public parks for picnics; and providing group-based transportation, such as vans that bring senior citizens or handicapped people to day centres.

Public safety and community welfare benefit from the introduction of 'thick' community policing that entails much more than merely getting police officers on the beat. This involves the community in setting priorities for the police and in overseeing their conduct. And it requires involving the police in conflict resolution and in the protection of the overall quality of life.[23]

All future building, street, neighborhood and town planning should provide for enhanced public safety and community building. Among the numerous possibilities are wider sidewalks, porches that abut sidewalks, gates that block traffic but not pedestrians and much more. (The British experiment in modern tower-block building during the 1970s, which decimated communities that had existed in many working class neighborhood, parallels similar calamitous projects in the United States.)

Currently in the UK there is no duty to inform local residents about repeat sexual offenders released into a community. When paedophiles, who have a very high recidivism rate, are released from jail and move into a neighbourhood, there should be a duty to inform communities. At the same time, communities should be warned against harassing these offenders. (While such a combination may sound utopian it has been approximated in the US state of Washington.)

Criminals who have paid their dues to society, served their sentences and led a legitimate life without any new arrests for ten years should have their rights fully restored and their records sequestered. Such records would be reopened before sentencing only if they have been reconvicted. In this way a Third Way society can foster repentance, leading to full restoration of former criminals to membership in the community.

Restorative justice programmes, especially for non-violent first-time offenders, work to the same purpose. Such a scheme has been pioneered by the Thames Valley Police, and should be extended to many other jurisdictions. In Thames Valley, first-time offenders are given the option of attending a conference with the victim of the offence, who comes along with family or friends. The meeting is mediated by an officer. The aim is to allow the victim to voice their pain and to get the offender to understand the consequences of their actions. The programme has been quite successful: during Thames Valley Police's initial three-year trial, the re-offending rate under restorative justice was reported to be 3 per cent, while the rate under the traditional caution is 35 per cent.[24]

3. Moral culture and its institutions

The power of the moral culture of communities

The primary social role of communities is often seen to be its fostering of interpersonal bonding, rather than its provision of moral culture. However, both have an important role in nourishing I-Thou relationships and in undertaking important social functions. While community bonding satisfies a profound human need, *moral culture can serve to significantly enhance social order while reducing the need for state intervention in social behaviour*. One should not allow legitimate ambivalence about the moral voices of communities (which will be addressed shortly) to overwhelm their tremendous potential contributions to good forms of social order.

There are clearly some forms of behaviour that a good society considers anathema and must seek to curb (such as damaging the environment, domestic violence, neglect of children, selling alcohol and cigarettes to minors). The moral culture of the community helps to define such behaviours. Most importantly, the community's ability to draw on subtle and informal processes of social regulation, such as approbation and censure, is much more compatible with ends-based relations than relying on the coercive powers of the state.

Extensive studies have demonstrated that these processes play a major role in curbing drug abuse, preventing petty crime and violation of the environment, and much else.[25] Aside from curbing anti-social behaviour, the moral culture of communities can also foster good conduct, including attending to one's children and elders, paying taxes, volunteering and many other pro-social activities.[26]

While one should not exaggerate the role that community forms of social regulation play in reducing serious crime, the considerable success of those already implemented shows both the value of mobilising communities on the side of social order and one way these reductions can be achieved much more extensively than has been done so far.

One of the main virtues of drawing on the informal regulation of communities to foster pro-social behaviour is that few if any public costs are exacted, and such processes are much more sensitive to subtle individual differences than official programmes.[27]

Third Way governments do best when they resist the rush to legislate good behaviour. When there is a valid need to modify behaviour, the state should realise that relying on informal community-based processes is preferable to relying on the law.[28]

Third Way governments should realise that legislation often numbs the moral conscience. When legislation is introduced in places where a moral culture *does* exist, the result frequently will be to diminish the moral voices of the community. For example, if the government were to mandate that alcoholics attend AA meetings, such meetings would become far less effective than those in which attendees participate because of their own inner developments and the encouragement of those close to them.

We have also learned from attempts to suppress divorce, abortions and consumption of alcohol by law that such policies tend to backfire and should be avoided, whether or not one opposes these behaviours. One should have faith in faith; the shortest line to pro-social conduct, whatever one considers such conduct to be, entails convincing people of the merits of the moral claims we lay on them. The law best follows new shared moral understandings rather than trying to lead them. The American Prohibition is a telling example of what happens when this point is ignored.

This is not to suggest that there is no room for legislation concerning moral and social issues. However, it is far better for informal social processes to underpin pro-social behaviour than for the police, courts and inspectors to do so. And laws that supplement and help sustain moral cultures will be more effective and humane than those that try to take the lead.

The difference between 'naked' laws (not preceded or backed by moral commitments) and 'well-covered' ones has major implications for public leaders and politicians. Leaders have two rather distinct roles. One, often underscored, is to prepare legislation and build support for it among the legislators. The other rather different and less well-understood role is to build up and change the moral culture. They best combine both attributes by leading with moral persuasion before they call on the legislature. Such leaders can carry their society much further along the Third Way.

Limiting the power of communities

While the moral cultures of communities are a major wellspring for constructing a good society, community-based morality itself needs to be scrutinised by members as well as outside observers. One method is to assess the community's moral culture by drawing on shared societal values as enshrined in the basic laws or the constitution of the state. Communities must be contained and balanced, just like all the other elements that make for a good society.[29]

While one may differ about specifics, in principle no community can be fully relied upon to determine that which is right and wrong. For example, should immigrant communities be allowed to arrange marriages even if there is a large age difference between the couple and consent is doubtful? Should female circumcision or child labour be tolerated? These are not questions over which communities should have the final say, as they concern basic human rights.

Communities in earlier ages, and even some in contemporary free societies, have oppressed individuals and minorities. It is the role of the state to protect the rights of all members in all communities as well as those of outsiders present within the communities' confines. Thus, no community should be allowed to violate the right to free speech, assembly and so on of anyone – whether the are members, visitors, passers-by or otherwise. Any notion that communities can be relied upon as the sole or final arbitrator of morality falls apart with the simple observation that a community may reach 100 per cent consensus in discriminating against some people on the basis of race. This vision of contained yet thriving communities is not far-fetched. Numerous communities exist within democratic societies that abide by their constitutions or basic laws. The rules that contain communities may be further extended or curtailed as constitutions are modified, but the basic principle is the same: *unfettered communities are no better than unfettered markets or states*. Third Way society achieves a balance through mutual containment of its core elements; the community is not exempted. However, the fact that communities can get out of hand should not be used as an argument against communities *per se*. Like medicine, food and drink, if taken in good measure communities are essential elements of the good life; if taken to excess, they can destroy it.

Rights and responsibilities

Some people champion individual and human rights and civil liberties as an unbounded principle, to which exceptions are to be tolerated only under very special conditions; others demand that people live up to their duties (whether prescribed by state or church), with very little concern for their rights. At the core of the Third Way ought to be the recognition that a good society combines respect for individual rights and fulfilment of basic human needs with the expectation that members live up to their responsibilities to themselves, their family and friends, and to the community at large.

One of the greatest achievements of the communitarian approach has been curbing the language of rights that has turned every want and interest into a legal entitlement, fostering unnecessary litigiousness.[30] While this is largely an American malaise, in the UK compensation claims have risen exponentially in the past ten years. In US 'rights talk', which fosters a disregard of social responsibility, was dominant in the 1980s, in the days of rampant individualism. Today, it has been largely replaced by a wide recognition that both individual rights and social responsibilities must be respected.[31]

What exactly is meant by 'rights *and* responsibilities'?

Basic individual rights are inalienable, just as one's social obligations cannot be denied. However, it is a grave moral error to argue that there are 'no rights without responsibilities', or vice versa.[32] Thus, a person who evades taxes, neglects their children or fails to live up to their social responsibilities in some other way is still entitled to a fair trial, free speech and other basic rights. The number of basic rights we should have may be debated, but those that are legitimate are not conditional.

Hence, policies that deny criminals the right to vote while in jail (as holds in both the UK and the US), some even after they have served their term (as is the case in many states in the US), should be modified. Following the same principle, nobody should be denied the basic necessities of life even if they have not lived up to their responsibilities, such as to find work. There are sufficient other ways to show our disapproval and punish irresponsible individuals if this is called for.

As a corollary, a person whose rights have been curbed – perhaps a person has been denied their right to vote because of a registration foul-up or jail sentence, or has been silenced through a meritless libel suit – is still not exempt from attending to their children, paying taxes, not littering and other social responsibilities.

In short, while rights and responsibilities are complementary and necessitate one another, each has their own moral standing and is part and parcel of ends-based relationships. A good society does not deny a person her basic rights even if she does not live up to her responsibilities, just as it does not exempt from responsibility those whose rights have not been fully honoured.

Responsibility from all, for all

Responsibilities *from all* means that a good person, a member of a good society, contributes to the common good. No one is exempt, although of course people will vary greatly in the contributions they can make. Consider a paraplegic who has lost the use of his limbs. He is permanently institutionalised. He uses a small stick in his mouth to turn pages of a book. Should we provide him with a nurse's aide to turn the pages or expect him to take that much responsibility for his own well-being? In order to serve both the person's dignity and the expectation that everyone will do as much for the common good as they can, we would expect him to turn the pages himself, assuming he can do so without undue effort. If assuming responsibility to the best of one's abilities applies under these circumstances, surely no one is exempt from contributing to the common good in line with their ability.

Accordingly, high school students should be encouraged to do community service as part of their civic practice, perhaps as 'millennium volunteers'.[33] Senior citizens should be expected to help each other, members of their families and their community. Those who receive welfare and cannot find gainful work should hold community jobs. People with contagious diseases should be expected to make special efforts not to spread it to others and so on.

The reference here is not primarily to legal commitments, enforced by courts and by the police, but to moral obligations.[34] And discharging one's responsibility should not be considered a sacrifice or a punishment but an ennobling activity, something a good person does. Indeed, high school students can gain deep satisfaction from working in soup kitchens, as senior citizens can by voluntarily running social centres for other seniors, and so on.

Responsibility from all is to be paralleled by responsibility *for all*. Responsibility for all means that everybody is to be treated with the respect due to all human beings. This means first of all social inclusion. Communities can play an especially important role in ensuring that everyone is included and treated with the full respect entitled to them by the fact of their humanity, treated as an end in themselves.[35] An obvious example is that discrimination based on race, ethnicity, gender, sexual preference, religious background or disability should be the focus of moral dissuasion and legally banned. Discrimination not only offends our elementary sense of justice – it is incompatible with treating people as ends in themselves.

Responsibility for all also means ensuring that everyone has access to the basic necessities of life. Voluntary associations, extended families, friends, mutual saving associations and religious charities can help to provide some of these, but cannot take on the final responsibility to ensure that all will be attended to. It is the responsibility of the state to ensure that such provisions are available to all.

In treating people as ends, Third Way societies must recognise that there are certain basic provisions that are everyone's due. These basics include food, shelter, clothing and healthcare. We should treat law-abiding members of the community at least as well as we treat prisoners of war and incarcerated criminals, all whom are granted said provisions.

No one's basic humanity and membership in the community should be denied. *It follows that no one should be completely cut off from welfare* or dumped into the streets even if they refuse to work, attend classes or do community service. The provisions to such idle or selfish people (who are a minority of benefits recipients) may be reduced and not include cash beyond some small amount, but the state's duty in a good society is to ensure that no one goes hungry, homeless, unclothed or sick and unattended. They may well deserve much more, and what is 'enough' – for instance in terms of healthcare – might be rather difficult to define.[36]

Similarly, there is considerable room for debate over what such a *rich basic minimum* entails.[37] That understanding is sure to differ with the economic conditions of the society, the age of those effected and their health status, and the community's specific moral shared understanding. But these deliberations ought to be about how extensive the provision of these basic good should be – not whether they should be provided at all.

Providing essentials to people will not kill the motivation to work for most, as long as work is available and they are able. And if there are some who abuse the system, a good society will consider this a small price to pay in order to not deny anyone's basic humanity. Putting mental patients, alcoholics, mothers with children or anyone else on to the streets, cutting off all benefits to them, is simply not compatible with these assumptions.

The further we advance along the Third Way, the more we must seek to abolish sources of social exclusion and snobbery. For the UK, public policy steps in this direction include abolishing the hereditary peers sitting in the second chamber of parliament, and not providing tax exemption for clubs practicing gender-based or racial discrimination. Given that class lines are not merely matters of economics and education but also part symbolism, appropriate gestures are also called for. As Prime Minister Blair put it: 'Liberate Britain from old class divisions. Remaining symbols and institutional support of class elitism should be actively discouraged or banned.' This and other such statements point to the need for further reform of the British education system given that its structure seems to support the continuation of class divisions.

The elitist university system is not compatible with a society based on merit and achievement. Admission to universities should be based not on parentage or public school pedigree, but on what they have and can accomplish. For starters, a sort of affirmative action programme should be introduced. It would cut off all direct and indirect taxpayer support to universities that admit highly disporpotionally from private schools. In 1999, for instance, Oxford admitted over half of its students from schools that accommodate only 7 per cent of secondary students nationally. Doubling the number of students admitted from all other schools should be a minimum target for the next five years. Oxford historian Andrew Roberts's recent comment about the Millennium Dome – 'It was designed for working-class people, not for the likes of me... It's staggeringly vulgar and common'[38] – bespeaks the existing prejudices that must be overcome.

Aside from advancing elementary fairness, opening access to top universities to all talents in the society at large is essential for a society that seeks to successfully embrace the knowledge economy.

Another issue is how progress might be signalled. As we are dealing partly in symbols, one place to start may be to bring back Harold Wilson's beer and sandwiches with working class people, rather than leaders limiting their outings to posh yuppie restaurants; more visits to road-side fast food restaurants and pubs rather than the Royal Opera House; and ensure that when honours are handed out, they are not skewed towards the upper classes.

In many areas there is a complex and tense relationship between rights and responsibilities. In these situations it is a grave mistake to presume that either rights or responsibilities are dominant. Rights and responsibilities should be treated as two cardinal moral claims. In the best of all worlds, both can be fully honoured. In reality, policies cannot often maximise both. But no *a priori* assumption should be made that priority will be given to one rather than the other.[39]

All policies that impinge on the balance between individual rights and social responsibilities should be reviewed and adjusted accordingly. So the right to privacy should be respected, but it should not take priority over protection of life and limb. For example, mandatory drug testing of school bus drivers and air traffic controllers is legitimate because in this case the violation of their privacy is limited while the danger to those they are entrusted with is considerable. At the same time, the ban on viewing of medical records by employers – records that concern the most intimate parts of our life and whose violation yields at best minimal social benefits – should be upheld and fully enforced.

A balanced society approaches the tension between individual rights and social responsibilities along these lines and adjusts its policies accordingly. In some areas it might enhance the reach of rights (for instance in the protection of personal information) while in others the claim of social responsibilities (for instance, keeping DNA profiles of all criminals), without such a combined approach being inconsistent. The same holds for increasing freedom of information, subjecting the police to race relations laws and the armed forces to human rights, as defined by the European Court of Human Rights, on the one hand, while also enabling police to intercept and decode email messages on the other. A good case in point is the recently enacted new surveillance powers of MI5. Along the same line, drug dealers in prisons should be stopped and routine testing of inmates should be introduced.

Moral dialogues: changing moral cultures

Debates about our moral culture are often unnecessarily polarised. We are not limited to either adhering to traditional conservative mores (for example, traditional two-parent families, with mothers at home) or treating all behaviours as if they had equal legitimacy (two parents, single parents, gay marriages, sequential monogamies, polygamy). We can express a preference for peer marriages (in which fathers and mothers have the same rights and the same responsibilities) over other forms of family without condemning the latter. There are social and moral options between rigidly sticking to tradition (as parts of the religious right demand) and a cultural-moral free-for-all (as some on the left have, in effect, advocated in the past).

While initially the moral culture of a given community or group of communities is handed down from generation to generation, this culture need not be fixed or 'traditional'. On the contrary, moral culture is continually recast to reflect new social needs, demands, insights and, above all, moral claims. This occurs through a process of special importance to those seeking a good society: moral dialogue. Moral dialogues are 'give and take' discussions that engage values rather than merely interests or wants. They involve more than facts and reasons; they engage our beliefs. They are composed of the many hours spent over meals, in pubs, while commuting, at work and in the media discussing moral issues.

Local communities, whole national societies and even international communities engage in extensive dialogues about acute moral issues, such as our duty to the environment, women's rights and sexual discrimination, and specific questions such as gay marriages, putting children on trial as adults, the death penalty, cruelty to animals and testing a whole village's DNA in order to catch a criminal.

Usually only one or two topics are the subject of intensive moral dialogue at any one time. Practically anyone can try to initiate a moral dialogue, from the prime minister to a local poet, from a media personality to a group of protesters. However, it is ultimately the public at large that decides which dialogues it will engage in. Despite claims to the contrary, the media – which serves as an important venue for moral dialogues – controls neither the agenda nor the outcome, although of course it influences both. This is because the media itself is not of one mind, and because the public is much less susceptible to brainwashing than is often assumed.[40]

Moral dialogues are largely about values. They are not dialogues among experts but among citizens. Moral dialogues often draw on factual and logical arguments, but they are mainly ethical, rather than empirical, in nature. Recall, for instance, the arguments that have taken place over bombing Serbia during the Kosovo war, releasing General Pinochet or banning fox-hunting.

When a community is engaged in a moral dialogue, the discussion often seems disorderly, meandering and endless. However, it frequently does lead to a genuine recasting of that community's voluntary moral culture, that which the community condones or censures.

Most importantly, *through the process of moral dialogue people often modify their conduct, feelings and beliefs.* For example, in the 1950s most communities had no sense of a moral obligation toward the environment. The profound moral dialogue that developed in the 1960s and 1970s led not merely to a shared moral sense of our duty to mother earth (although communities continue to differ on what exactly that entails) but also to a fair measure of changed behaviour, such as voluntary recycling and conservation of energy. *As a whole, if a community needs to change its social fabric in a significant way, moral dialogues are necessary to generate changes in personal and social conduct, and to underpin public policies.*

Moral dialogues can follow what British sociologists called 'moral panic' but these two should not be conflated. Panic alarms people and can lead them to embrace dubious policies. In contrast, moral dialogues lead them to re-examine their beliefs, world views and prejudices, and to recast them.

One of the great weaknesses of some Third Way governments is their tendency to take shortcuts, often skirting or short-changing the need for moral dialogue. For instance, the release of a Third Way framework document in Germany in mid-1998 by Chancellor Gerhard Schroeder was not preceded by a dialogue with the members of the Social Democratic Party or even its leadership, not to mention the German public at large. In contrast, changing Clause IV of the Labour party platform followed 'the widest consultation exercise ever undertaken by a British political party.... Tens of thousands took part, almost half the party participated'.[41]

Currently moral dialogues are badly needed in the UK on issues such as limiting the centrifugal effects of devolution, deeper involvement in the European Union, the implications of continued immigration and the effects of growing multiculturalism on the core values of the society. The rise of right-wing parties in Austria, Switzerland, Germany and France, and the romanticisation of Communist regimes in eastern Germany, are in part driven by lack of sufficient dialogue on these matters.

Another topic that calls for a moral dialogue is the scope and limits of Britain's international humanitarian efforts. What are the limits and scope of foreign aid? When should economic sanctions be applied? When is the exercise of force justified? When is it appropriate to cancel the debt of developing nations? Should we put pressure on other countries to change their moral cultures in matters ranging from child labour to female circumcision?

While there are no guaranteed ways to trigger moral dialogues or ensure their development, devices such as extensive public hearings by Parliamentary committees and inquiries by citizen commissions may initiate dialogue. The latter have no official standing and may be established by a think tank, foundation or some other civic body. They are composed of the representatives of major segments of society affected by the issues under study, conduct public hearings and publish recommendations based on the dialogue they trigger. Such devices must be used much more extensively if more people are to become further engaged by the moral and political issues at the heart of the Third Way.

Many groups that are strongly committed to specific values tend to demand that public leaders push their agenda through, engineering public support if it does not exist. The power of leadership in a democratic society is, thankfully, much more limited. Political leadership in free societies must judiciously choose occasions on which major changes are sought, with new coalitions built and political capital put at risk, rather than vainly tilting with the wind.

Such willingness to assume risk at select points was evident when Old Labour transformed into New Labour, when the old opposition between left and right was leapfrogged on the road to a Third Way. It is evident in the continued recasting of the welfare state, and in guiding Britain from an industrial to a knowledge-based economy. It will be called upon again to face the next major challenges of the Third Way: curbing inequality; balancing devolution with building a community of communities; and defining the place of the British community within the European one, among others.

Involving the public more in dialogues about major policy changes, especially those concerning moral and social issues, makes it more difficult to govern. Such dialogues are time-consuming and do not necessarily conclude as government may wish. But it is doubtful that it would be possible to achieve profound and lasting social change without such dialogues. To put it more starkly: a government can make incremental changes year on year without profoundly engaging the public – or it can truly lead in new directions. This can only be done if the public has been engaged and won over – often entailing significant changes in the direction government was seeking to move. After all, democracy entails much more than a solid majority in the parliament.

Family: the need for a definitive new look
Throughout history, in all societies, families have been entrusted with initiating character formation, introducing younger generations to the moral culture of the community, preparing them to be good people.

Before one can settle any of the numerous specific issues that arise from the transition from traditional forms of families to 'postmodern' ones, we require a more conclusive examination of the evidence about the effects of highly divergent social arrangements. To proceed, the government should convene a 'science court,' an inquiry composed of expert social scientists.[42] The court would hold public hearings, interrogating scientific witnesses and representatives of the various bodies of thought on the subject. The court might require additional analysis of existing data or the generation of new data, to provide a strong and shared body of relevant evidence. In this way it should be able to reach solid credible conclusions about critical issues that arise concerning our ability to replace the two-parent family, and help move to settle the public dialogue on these issues. Clearly it makes a great deal of difference for the moral culture and for public policy whether children suffer greatly or actually benefit, as some maintain, from new forms of family arrangements and the institutionalisation of children.

The science court should focus on children of young age, especially from birth until five, the years in which many believe the foundations of character are formed.

The science court should investigate not merely whether the parenting deficit is harmful, but also the implications of a growing 'children deficit'. There is evidence that the birth rate in many Third Way societies is falling below the population replacement level, with numerous ill consequences for society.[43] To put it more sharply, if we once held that the first social duty of the family is the moral education of children, it may now be – to have children.[44] Millions now see children as a burden, interfering with their careers and lifestyle. This is just another disconcerting reflection of the pressures of globalism and radical individualism.

The introduction of several new family policies might best be delayed until the work of the science court is completed. This holds, for instance, for legal authorisation of new forms of marriage,[45] such as time-limited commitments, giving full legal endorsement to household partnerships, and introducing covenant marriages.[46]

There are those who ask – why do we have to rule which form of marriage we ought to favour rather than let each person make her or his own choices? Firstly, as long as marriage remains a state sanctioned and enforced institution, we must decided what amounts to a marriage. The same is true for the question of who is entitled to benefits available to those who are married. Secondly, even if all state involvement was abolished, the science court would still be needed to help focus the moral debate, which reshapes voluntary moral culture. If one form or another of marriage and family were to prove harmful to children, we should not necessarily ban it, but families and communities ought at least to know about it.

Some key matters, though, require no study or inquiry. There should be no return to 'traditional' forms of family, in which women were treated as second class citizens. This would violate the principle of treating all as ends.[47] Fathers and mothers should have the same rights and responsibilities. Fathers obviously can look after children and women work outside of the household. A substantive step in the right direction will be made when laws that allow mothers of newborn children to take paid leave and have their jobs held for them for a given number of years are also fully applied to fathers.

There is no one correct way for work and family to be balanced; each person and couple need to work this out. It is, however, in the interest of a good society to encourage and enable parents to spend more time with their children.

Schools as places of character formation

Much has been written about making schools into more effective tools for the competitive information economy, and on the need to improve the academic skills and knowledge of graduates. However, we have also known since Aristotle about the importance of character development. In our society, schools are the places in which the character of young people is developed. They are the places people learn, or at least ought to, how to control their impulses and develop empathy, essential for treating one another as ends rather than only as instruments. They are the place where young people should learn how to deal civilly with one another and to resolve conflicts peacefully. Most importantly, in schools young people learn that treating others only as instruments is profoundly unethical, and that they have responsibilities for one another, their family and the community.

A good society requires good people; it cannot allow for character education to be driven out by academics. The direct experiences and narratives offered by schools are more important for character formation than lectures on ethics or civics. Community service, peer mentoring and other ways of taking responsibility, role playing and participation in mock governments are all vastly superior forms of civic education than formal and abstract lectures about democratic government.

To ensure that this core education principle will be heeded, an annual assessment should be made in all schools of the educational (as distinct from teaching) messages they impart, and of their approach to character formation. If these are defective, schools should be helped by personnel especially dedicated to this issue to restructure their approach.

Educational, family and welfare policies are often developed in isolation from one another and, most of all, from work practices. But if people are to be treated as ends, they cannot be viewed as fragments, as students *or* parents *or* workers. Each individual must be treated as a whole. This, in turn, requires a much better dovetailing of different policies. For example, school days end before most parents finish work. Unsurprisingly, a high level of juvenile crime occurs between 3 and 6pm. Gaps like these must be bridged with policies that treat the many aspects of society as segments of one whole.

4. The other partners: state and market

The good society is a partnership of three sectors – government, private sector, and community. Each one reflects and serves a distinct facet of our humanity. Only by serving all three, rather than fragmenting them or setting one against the other, can we achieve a society that encompasses the whole person, essential for their being treated as ends in themselves.

While these partners may differ in terms of their respective roles, and these may change with social conditions, in a good society the three sectors seek to cooperate with one another. Each is part of the solution; none is blamed as the source of the problem. They are complementary rather than antagonistic. Most importantly, each partner helps contain the others, to ensure one will not usurp the missions best accomplished by the others. Maintaining this three-way balance is at the heart of the good society.

The state
The Third Way approach maintains that sweeping and detailed control of the economy and society by the state is incompatible with a good society, as is an unfettered market. It also follows that while the state can and should be slimmed down, there are many tasks that are its legitimate domain.

i.   The main responsibility for public safety should rest with the state. Therefore, to the extent that the society draws on private policing (such as hired guards) and profit-making prisons, their conduct should be closely regulated.[48] At the same time, the state's function in this arena should be contained by the community. For instance, civil review boards can help ensure that the police do not brutalise citizens. Another form of containment is scrutiny by a free press.

ii. Citizens should not be armed in a good society, and police arms should be minimal. The state should ensure the continued disarmament of the population. To the extent that a civil militia is needed, as the Swiss hold for instance, arms are best deposited in public armories. Holding a gun up to a person is about as far as one can get from treating people as ends.

iii. A major goal for the next decade should be to significantly increase *certitude* (sometimes referred to as 'celerity') that those who violate the law will be caught, those caught will be convicted and those convicted will serve their term. An increase in certitude would allow a reduction in the length of prison terms and in the harshness of the term (for example, less solitary confinement and less reliance on high security prisons) while at the same time enhancing public safety. The result is a more humane treatment of criminals and greater possibility of their rehabilitation, in line with our criteria for the good society, as well as significantly lower public costs (after a transition period).[49]

Punishing those who violate the law is unavoidable in an orderly and just society. Increased certitude combined with shorter sentences will ensure punishment and curtail the inhuman and costly treatment that often ensues when people are incarcerated. Hopefully such an approach would also deter criminals more effectively.

iv. The state should be responsible for public health, that is, for health matters that are in the interest of the community: for example, the containment of communicable diseases, ensuring the safety of drugs and foods, and undertaking some forms of preventive health such as mandatory vaccinations and water fluoridation.

Illness and the resulting dependency not only exact increasingly large public costs, but are also incompatible with people achieving their full potential. Preventive care is the best antidote. Specific goals for preventive care should be set for each decade, including contributions expected from citizens, for instance, by increasing the amount of exercise they take. *Decreasing the rate of smoking, especially among teenagers, is the single most important preventive goal for the next ten years.* While figures differ, the importance of preventive care is highlighted by the finding that in a given period in the United States changes in lifestyle added 11.5 years to life expectation while improvements in medical services added only 0.5 years.

v.   A good society should view the market as akin to nuclear energy: it can provide an enormous and growing bounty of products and services, and help to serve the common good, including culture and arts, science and education, public health and welfare. However, it must be watched over carefully. If excessively restricted the market cannot perform well. At the same time, a good society assumes that if the market is not properly contained, it may dehumanise people and wreak havoc on local communities, families and social relations. Indeed, unfettered markets can undo I-Thou relations and allow I-It ones to dominate.

The Third Way does not lead to a free market any more than it favours football without rules or referees. The market has always operated within a social context, which has included a fabric of social values, laws and regulatory mechanisms. The role of the government is not to abolish these but to adapt them to changing conditions, especially to the cyber-age.

The main question Third Way societies struggle with is when to allow market forces a free rein and when to put up containing walls. (An obvious example of an area the market must be kept from penetrating is the distribution of transplantable human organs.) There are significant differences among Third Way societies on this viewpoint, which reflects how much progress they have made on this journey, especially between societies that have been Thatcherised (mainly the US and the UK) and those that have not travelled far down this road. However, *all Third Way societies should be much clearer about the areas into which market forces must be prevented from intruding. This is essential if the proper balance between the instrumental realm and that of ends is to be achieved and sustained.*

Third Way societies are currently making numerous incremental changes that favour market forces. These include greater flexibility in work rules, lower personal, capital gains and corporate tax rates, lower benefits, higher co-insurance charges, further privatisation, enabling firms to issue shares to their workers, enabling workers to purchase shares tax free, reforms of insolvency and much else.

Such changes will remain unnecessarily threatening and unprincipled as long as it is not clearly indicated which social boundaries will not be breached. Especially significant on this matter is the question of whether people can reliably assume that whatever the changes in economic policy, they will still have secure safety nets protecting their basic health insurance, retirement income and subsistence. Can people take for granted that even if these nets were set at lower levels, no one would be allowed to fall through them? Will work be available for all those who seek it or are pressured to find employment? Will the income from work be sufficient to keep people out of poverty? If not, will it be supplemented along the lines of the Working Families Tax Credit? Will training be available for those made redundant by technologically driven changes? While details can be debated, *people in a good society are accorded a basic sense of economic security.*

Markets cannot be free from public oversight and regulation. To a limited extent one can and should rely on the market to self-regulate (for instance, industries agreeing not to target young children in their advertising) and communities can play a containing role. For example, many UK consumer groups play an important role as unofficial 'watchdogs' of corporate behaviour. But experience shows that the main responsibility for containing the market must rest with the state. To ensure that state regulations do not become excessive, they should remain in effect only if examinations show that they do not unnecessarily restrain the market or that they cannot be replaced by better regulations or other ways of achieving the same social purposes.

vi. The notion that cyberspace can be a new utopian world, free from state controls, in which people govern themselves, is without reality or justice. Cyberspace has long since turned from a virtual village into a metropolis in which people need protection. As the proportion of transactions conducted in cyberspace continues to increase, so must public oversight. Prescription drugs sold on the internet cannot be free from the protections that customers require offline. Taxes cannot be avoided. Messages transmitted by drug lords, paedophiles and terrorists cannot be exempt from the reach of the law. Libel on the internet is not different from any other.

Some controls can be exerted by parents and educators. Others can rely on self-regulation and transparency (for example, the posting of privacy policies and the use of trustmarks). However, increasingly the virtual world will become like the rest of the world, and will need the same careful balance of freedom and public scrutiny.

While the basic need for containing cyberspace's economic and technological forces is the same as in other markets, the tools may well be different. Because cyberspace knows no national borders, development of worldwide agreements and enforcement must be achieved as rapidly as possible.

Ensuring basic access for all is another role for the state, so that cyberspace does not become another arena for social exclusion. This will be especially important as more education and voting takes place in virtual formats.

vii. Given the close association between work and a sense of self-worth, which is a vital foundation of ends-based relationships, public policy should aim both to hold inflation at bay and also to stimulate the economy, enabling higher growth in general and low unemployment especially. Given recent evidence that higher growth and lower unemployment than previously considered possible can be achieved without rekindling serious inflation, and given the inhumanity of joblessness even in a state with broad welfare provisions, public policy should tilt more toward growth and less toward inflation fighting. An annual growth rate above 3 per cent and an unemployment rate below 5 per cent should be considered realistic targets.

Expanding available work through the market until unemployment is low is the most desirable outcome. However, to the extent that this is impractical, policies which distribute available work are preferable to those that protect job privileges but keep unemployment high (for instance, by curbing part-time work). Surely it is better for all who seek and are able to work to be employed than for some to have high salaries and benefits well protected, only to be highly taxed in order to pay unemployment benefits to those who are kept out of the labour market. The Dutch approach to employment is closer to an ends-respecting model than that of several other Third Way countries.[50]

As a last resort, community jobs should be available for all those who cannot find gainful work in the marketplace or public sector.[51] These could include environmental improvements and teaching aides, as well as other work that would not be carried out if it had to be paid for. Thus, community jobs would not compete with other forms of job creation or with those who hold low-paying jobs.

viii. The state should be attentive to environmental needs and coordinate those activities needed to shore up the environment, but it should not shoulder them all.[52] To some extent environmental protection can be reconciled with market interests, and become a source of new jobs and technological innovation. At the same time, the state in a good society recognises our duty to pass on the environment to our children in good or better condition than we inherited it, and that such a social commitment entails some net public costs.

These costs can be reduced as people increasingly recognise that protecting the environment is a part of everyone's social moral responsibilities, an important source of community jobs and a place for volunteering.[53]

ix. To help sustain the three-way partnership, the state fosters communities where they exist and helps prime their development where they have failed. It is careful not to contribute to their ossification and decay by pre-empting their role. Hence, as a rule the state should not be the first source of social services. Small loans, child-care, sick care, counselling and much else is best provided in the first instance by members of the immediate and extended family, local and other communities, voluntary associations, workplaces and others. When the state becomes the first or sole source of these services, it undermines, demoralises and bureaucratises relationships that are at the core of communal life.

In order to encourage communities' role in social services, all state agencies should have *citizen participation advisory boards*. Their task would be to find ways for citizens to participate as volunteers in delivering some services currently carried by the state. They should also play a role in providing timely, relevant and informed feedback on the performance of service providers.

The state should foster economic and social entrepreneurship, and therefore not impose taxes or regulations which disable the economic engines of innovation and change. At the same time, *taxes should not disadvantage those who labour in favour of those who invest.* If taxes are withheld at source, they should be withheld from both workers and investors.[54] (Because of the dangers of capital flight, to proceed may well require carrying this measure out on the level of the EU, or most likely the OECD.)

The private sector

'We are not against market-based economy but market-based society.'

Lionel Jospin, Prime Minister of France

Third Way societies recognise that the market is the best engine for production of goods and services, for work and thus jobs, for economic progress. Moreover, the private sector may foster innovation that adapts the economy to changing conditions and opportunities.

While much attention is properly paid to social problems created by market forces – factory closures, loss of job security, overwork in some industries and idleness in others – such problems should not blind us to the basic merit of strong economic growth. So, for example, rising international trade raises a host of problems concerning labour and environmental standards, but we should also recognise that trade, in the long run, benefits most societies and most members of society.

Those who lose their jobs as a result should be helped by the community and the state. Policies such as the United States' Trade Adjustment Assistance (providing targeted support for those dislocated by economic change) should be increased, allowing redundant workers to be retrained and, if necessary, resettled, or given community jobs.[55]

Some claim that most social standards must be suspended for a nation to be able to compete in the global economy. While some adaptations are necessary, each should be critically examined. It is empirically incorrect and morally false to assume that a society cannot respond to the negative effects of globalisation, or that, if it could respond, the loss of economic efficiency would *a priori* not be worth paying.

It is equally important to recognise that globalisation calls for the development of national, regional and global social and political institutions. As corporations and internet businesses increasingly become cross-national and global forces, so balancing groups – from labour unions to environmentalists – must link arms across national lines, and regulatory and other public institutions must be regional and global in scope. Limits on violations of the environment, land mines, trade in ivory and much else are preliminary and rather weak examples, but they point to what must be done.

The art of combination

Third Way imagery often conceals the fact that social goods are commonly achieved by hybrids, in which two or three sectors come together, creating organisations that are often superior to single sector ones.[56] The merits and problems of these hybrids require further attention. The unsatisfactory results of British railway privitisation and of efforts to create private universities should convince us of the need for such examination.

There is no one 'correct' form of combination. In some areas, private–public partnerships work best, in others public authorities do so, in still others the state may need to be reintroduced.[57]

Categories of hybrids include:

i.   Religious institutions and voluntary associations that provide social services – financed in part by the government.

ii.   Privately run or not-for-profit cultural institutions (universities, museums, theatres and so on) whose initial capital costs and/or start-up funds are provided by the state (which may also continue to provide some partial subsidies) but which draw mainly on their operating funds, some capital outlays, donations and extra income from their gift shops, restaurants and so on.
iii. State vouchers that allow people to purchase community services or market products, for instance, housing allowances and pre-school childcare.
iv.   Public authorities, like the BBC, are especially important as commercial forms of communication become more influential. A credible plan for strengthening the BBC is through establishing a mutual society in which ownership of the public service broadcaster would be granted to licence-fee payers in the general public.

There is much more scope for combinations in matters concerning utilities (especially water), public services (the London Underground) and many others. Let us swear off the simplistic market-or-government dichotomy.

The knowledge society and curtailing scarcity

Much has been stated, correctly, about the importance of fostering the transition to a knowledge-based economy. Such a transformation – which entails prioritising investment in people (via education and life-long learning) as well as technology – is said to be essential for prosperity. It could also be a good way to reduce menial labour and increase the number of jobs that are stimulating, family friendly and compatible with the needs of the environment. However, *surprisingly little attention has been paid to an attribute of a knowledge-based economy that by itself justifies heavy investment in it: its potential to reduce scarcity and enhance social justice.*

Knowledge as a resource differs greatly from those relied upon in industrial societies – material goods, capital goods, from steel to petrol – in that it can be *shared and consumed* many times over. Thus, if a factory uses a ton of steel, this steel is no longer available to any other user and, as a result, issues of resource allocation and scarcity arise. However, when a person puts a design on the internet – for a better mousetrap, car, home, software programme or whatever – millions can use it and the originator still has the original.[58] Similarly, many thousands of people can download a piece of music, poetry or film and it can still be consumed again. While not all knowledge is or can be shared in this manner, a growing number of new 'goods' are being shared on the internet in this way.

Of course, there are tricky problems that must be worked out concerning intellectual property and patent rights. However, one should not overlook that there are very large bodies of knowledge that can be shared legally in this fascinating new way – including numerous books, music and art for which the copyright has expired and that are in the public domain. The same should hold for most information produced by the government, from national statistics to text of parliamentary debates.

The more people satisfy their wants by drawing on free knowledge, say by reading downloaded files, playing chess on the internet or joining virtual self-help groups, the scarcer scarcity becomes and the smaller the I-It sector a society must bear. Scarcity will never be eliminated. However, the more people (once their basic material wants are sated) draw on open sources of knowledge (including culture), the more ends based their relations can become.

Last but not least, there is a profound connection between fostering the knowledge-based economy and enhancing social justice. Most earlier theories of justice are based on the idea of transferring large amounts of resources from the haves to the have-nots. This raises obvious political difficulties. However, to the extent that those whose basic needs are met draw their additional satisfaction from non-scarce resources, the door opens to a whole new world, in which the well-off may well be less opposed to the transfer of material goods to the less well-off. And those who have less could benefit from non-scarce knowledge resources, once the community and state ensure that they have the basic skills and resources needed to access the new world of knowledge.

This may seem far-fetched, visionary and utopian. Yet while such a world may be in our distant future, its harbingers are all around us. The more we foster a transition to a knowledge-based economy and basic access for all, the closer we come to living in a society that is driven less by scarcity – and is more equitable as a result.

Limiting corruption

Few issues concerning the proper balance between market and state are more important than preventing those with economic power from also concentrating political power. In numerous free societies, there is a growing stream of private monies into public hands – either in the old-fashioned form of bribery or in the modern form of special interests 'contributing' funds to political parties, legislators or government officials in exchange for special treatment at the public's cost. Few developments are more corrosive for the Third Way than the corruption of public institutions. Such double-fisted concentration of power violates a profound precept of a truly democratic society, whereby all members are equal citizens, whatever their wealth differences.

Trust is a key element of ends-based relationships; while general social trust among the general public has been diminishing, trust in public leaders and institutions is particularly vulnerable. The American public has become rather cynical of a political system in which limiting the role of private monies in public life is almost impossible. European societies must pay more attention to this matter than they have hitherto. While the problem may well be less severe in the UK than in many other societies, the best time to lock the barn is before the horse is stolen. Several new laws and regulations in the UK seek to curb the corruption of politics – these include banning foreign funding and paid questions, declaring all interests in a public register and publicising donations to political parties over £2,000. It remains to be seen whether these will suffice to protect public life from private monies.[59]

5. Sustaining the community of communities

Devolution coupled with nation building

The Labour government has lived up to its promise of devolution. However, the process has revealed a slew of new issues to be addressed. One concerns ways to devolve further 'down', bringing power closer to the people, to the level of communities rather than regions such as Scotland and Wales, or even cities as large as London. If devolution is extended downward, citizens will have more opportunities to participate in their own government, and are more likely to become politically engaged.

A more urgent challenge is learning to devolve power while reinforcing the loyalties and bonds that maintain a national society. The mere mention of Scottish independence, and the intense squabbles between regions over variations in central government funding, are indications that this issue requires urgent attention.

A strong economy, reallocation of wealth, sound environmental programmes and respect for basic laws can only be advanced if smaller communities are parts of more encompassing ones. England or Scotland alone could not achieve the kind of international leadership and economic power Britain currently provides. In the current environment, nations cannot avoid fragmentation without active leadership and concrete society-building measures.

The quest for such measures is, for the most part, yet to be undertaken. Forming nationwide work groups, projects and programmes that cut across regional borders – for example, economic development programmes encompassing northeast England and southern Scotland – might serve this end. Changing the National Curriculum to include more historical material focusing on the achievements of the union and less on civil wars might help. Honouring those who foster unity rather than separateness would be useful. But these alone will not suffice. Much new thinking is still required on this issue.

The vision of society as a community of communities applies to geographic , racial and ethnic communities alike. A good society thrives on a diversity of cultures that enriches people's lives through the arts, music, dance, social contact, cuisine and much more. But such a multi-cultural society cannot flourish without a shared framework, which itself will evolve over time. Its elements include commitment to a democratic way of life, to basic laws or the constitution, to mutual respect and, above all, to the responsibility to treat all others as ends in themselves. Diversity should not become the opposite of unity, but should exist *within* unity.

Sustaining a given community of communities does not contradict the gradual development of more encompassing communities, such as the European Union or, eventually, a world community. These too will be composed of networks of communities rather than hundreds of millions of individuals, or even hundreds of fragmented social entities. It is foolish to believe that the collapse of nations does not matter because the fragments may then join the larger European community in what Philip Dodd refers to as 'the Euro-federalist solution to the present battle over Britain.'[60] Such notions are unduly optimistic about the pace and scope of Europe's development as a true community. They disregard the fact that more encompassing communities are not composed of numerous small fragments: they are an additional layer of community, rather than one that pre-empts the others.

Finally, deeper involvement in the EU is best preceded by extensive moral dialogues, not merely one referendum about the euro. While there seems to be considerable support for joining a European community, below the surface there are strong euro-sceptical sentiments that must be taken seriously.

Limiting inequality

Society cannot sustain itself as a community of communities if disparities in well-being and wealth between elites and the rest of society are too great. While we may debate exactly what social justice entails, there is little doubt what community requires. If some members of a community become further removed from the daily living conditions of most other members – leading lives of hyper-affluence in gated communities, with chauffeured limousines, servants and personal trainers – they lose contact with the rest of the community. Such isolation not only frays social bonds and insulates privileged people from the moral cultures of the community, but it also blinds them to the realities of their fellow citizens' lives. This in turn may cause them to favour unrealistic policies ('let them eat cake'), which further undermine the community's trust in them.

To prevent this problem it has been suggested that the state should provide equality of outcomes. However, during the twentieth century we have learned that this treatment goes against the grain of a free society. As a result, even command and control societies have been unable to truly implement this approach. We also learned that, when it is approximated, it undermines creativity, excellence and motivation to work, and is unfair to those who do apply themselves. Furthermore, the resulting labour costs are so high as to render a society uncompetitive in the global economy.

Equality of opportunity has been extolled as a substitute. However, to ensure equality of opportunity for all, everyone must have similar a starting point. *These can be provided only if all are accorded certain basics,* which we have already established is a core part of treating all as ends and not merely as means.

This volume focuses on the future rather than assessing the past. One should note that major steps in the right direction have already been undertaken by the Blair government. Economic growth is high, which helps the poor and not merely those who are well off. A minimum wage has been introduced and unemployment is at a 19-year low. A budget deficit has been licked and expenditure on health and education have been significantly increased, after many years of cuts or stagnant spending.

Additional policies to further curb inequality can be made to work at both ends of the scale. Special education efforts to bring children from disadvantaged backgrounds up to par, such as Surestart (in the UK) and Head Start (in the US), and training workers released from obsolescent industries for new jobs, are examples of programmes providing a measure of equality of outcome to make equality of opportunity possible. However, the results often reveal themselves very slowly. Hence in the shorter run greater effects will be achieved by raising the Working Families Tax Credit and the minimum wage and by creating initiatives that encourage sharing of resources between communities.

Raising the minimum wage invites the criticism that people will be priced out of the jobs market. However, if the level of minimum wage is tied to what people need to provide for their basic needs, it is the moral obligation of a good society to provide for this standard of living. The only alternative to a proper minimum wage would be welfare payments – which tend to be degrading, develop dependency and are more politically unattractive than minimum wage. However, it does not follow that the minimum wage should automatically be tied to a *relative* poverty line – one that rises as quickly as other wages in society. A rich basic minimum is defined in absolute terms, not as a statistical artifact.

For a long time it has been known that the poor will be with us, even if they work, as long as they have no assets. People who own assets, especially a place of residence (whether or house or a flat), are more likely to 'buy' into a society, to feel that they are part of the community and to be an active member of it. *One major way to advance home ownership is through schemes that allow those on low incomes to obtain mortgages,* as provided in the United States by federally chartered corporations such as Fannie Mae. More should to be done on this front.

We suggest that this might be achieved by following the same model used in Earned Income Tax Credit in the United States and Working Families Tax Credit in the UK: *providing low income people with earned interest on mortgages.* Those whose income is below a certain level may earn, say, £2 for every £1 they set aside to provide them with the seed money for a buying a home. Alternatively, 'sweat' equity might be used as the future owner's contribution, for instance if they work on their housing site.

While raising the income and ownership of the poor might ensure that everybody can afford the basic minimum essential to the core principle of a good society, such measures will not suffice for the purposes of community building. Other measures that prevent ever-higher levels of inequality should be undertaken if wealthier people are not to become too distanced from the rest of society.

Such measures may include maintaining progressive taxation from most if not all sources, increasing inheritance tax and ensuring that tax on capital is paid as it is on labour. Given that such measures cannot be adopted if they seriously endanger the competitive status of a country, they would be difficult to implement solely at the national level. A number of inequality curbing measures may well require co-introduction or harmonisation at least within the EU and preferably with the OECD countries; better yet (in the long term) worldwide.

Ultimately this matter, as with many others, will not be properly addressed until there is a sea-change in the moral culture of society and the purposes that animate it. Major reallocation of wealth cannot be forced by a democratic society, and vigorous attempts to impose it will cause a flight of wealth and damage the economy in other ways. In contrast, history from early Christianity to Fabian socialism teaches us that people who share proper values will be inclined to voluntarily share some of their wealth. A good society seeks to promote such values through a wide-ranging moral dialogue.

6. The next grand dialogue: A moderate return of counterculture?

The good society understands that ever-increasing levels of material goods are not a reliable source of human well-being and contentment, let alone of a morally sound society. It recognises that the pursuit of well-being through ever higher levels of consumption is Sisyphian. This is not an argument in favour of poverty and self-denial. However, extensive data shows that, once basic material needs are well-sated and securely provided, additional income does not add to happiness.[61] The evidence shows that profound contentment is found in nourishing relationships, in bonding, in community building and public service, and in cultural and spiritual pursuits. Capitalism never aspired to address the needs of the whole person; at best it treats a person as an economic entity. Statist socialism subjugated rather than inspired people. It is left to good societies to fill the void.

The most profound problems that plague modern societies will be fully addressed only when those whose basic needs have been met shift their priorities up Maslow's scale of human needs. That is, only after they accord a higher priority to gaining and giving affection, cultivating culture, becoming involved in community service and seeking spiritual fulfilment. Such a shift in priorities is also required before we can truly come into harmony with the environment, as these higher priorities replace material consumption. Such a new set of priorities may also be the only conditions under which the well-off would support serious reallocation of wealth and power, because their personal fortunes would no longer be based on amassing ever larger amounts of consumer goods.[62] In addition, the change would free millions of people, gradually one hopes all of them, to relate to each other as members of families and communities. This sea-change would lay the social foundations for a society in which ends-based relations dominate while instrumental ones are well-contained and gradually curtailed.

This shift in priorities – a return to a sort of moderate counterculture, or a turn to voluntary simplicity – requires a grand dialogue about our personal and shared goals. Intellectuals and the media can help launch such a dialogue and model the new forms of behaviour. Public leaders can nurse the recognition of these values by moderating consumption and by celebrating those whose achievements are compatible with the good society rather than with a merely affluent one. But ultimately, such a shift lies in changes in the hearts and minds, in the values and conduct, of us all. We shall not travel far toward a good society unless such a dialogue is launched and developed to a positive conclusion.

Notes

1. 'Goldilocks Politics', *The Economist*, 19 December 1998.

2. Teles SM, 'An Apologia for the Third Way'. Paper presented at a recent American Political Science Association convention.

3. Elizabeth Frazer, Official Fellow, Tutor, and Lecturer in Politics at the University of Oxford, has written that 'Tony Blair's communitarianism was influenced by the philosophy of John MacMurray.' Frazer E, 1999, *The Problems of Communitarian Politics*, Oxford University Press, London, 25.

4. On this point see 'The Slippy Centre', Chait J 1998, *The New Republic*, 16 November, 19.

5. Gray J, 1996, *After Social Democracy: Politics, capitalism and the common life*, Demos, London, 16.

6. According full attention to the importance of communities is what is most lacking on the Third Way, which otherwise retraces quite closely new communitarian thinking. On communitarianism see Etzioni A, 1993, *The Spirit of Community*, Simon and Schuster, New York; Etzioni A, 1996, *The New Golden Rule*, Basic Books, New York; Tam H, 1998, *Communitarianism*, New York University Press; Gray, 1996 (note 5); Giddens A, 1998, *The Third Way*, Polity Press, Cambridge; Selznick P, 1992, *The Moral Commonwealth*, University of California Press, Berkeley; The Communitarian Network Web Site: <http://www.gwu.edu/~ccps>.

7. Stuster J, 1996, *Bold Endeavors: Lessons from polar and space exploration*, Naval Institute Press, Annapolis, Maryland, 8.

8. See for instance, Altman I, 1973, 'An ecological approach to the functioning of socially isolated groups,' in *Man in Isolation and Confinement*, Aldine Publishing Co, Chicago, 241-70; Barabaz AF, 1984, 'Antarctic isolation and imaginative involvement: Preliminary findings,' *International Journal of Clinical and Experimental Hypnosis*, no 32, 296-300; Johnson R, 1976, *Culture and Crisis in Confinement*, Lexington Books, Lexington, Massachusetts; Harrison AA et al, 1991, *From Antarctica to Outer Space: Life in isolation and confinement*, Springer-Verlag, New York.

9. Srole L et al, 1962, *Mental Health in the Metropolis: The midtown Manhattan study*, McGraw-Hill, New York.

10. Walz M, 1994, *Social Isolation and Social Mediators of the Stress of Illness*, Lit Verlag, Hamburg, Germany, 56-57.

11. Putnam RD, 2000, *Bowling Alone: The collapse and revival of American community*, Simon and Schuster, New York, 328; Berkman LF and Glass T, 2000, 'Social Integration, Social Networks, Social Support, and Health,' in Berkman LF and Kawachi I, eds, *Social Epidemiology*, Oxford University Press, New York, 137-174.

12. Hurley ML and Schiff L 1996, 'This town made wellness a way of life,' *Business and Health*, vol 14, no 12, 39-43. Accessed on http://proquest.umi.com/ on 31 March 2000.

13. Ibid.

14. Ibid.

15. Luke JS and Neville KR, 1998, 'Curbing Teen Pregnancy: A divided community acts together,' *The Responsive Community*, vol 8, no 3, 62-72.

16. The reason for this is that social

services are labour intensive, and labour costs rise more rapidly than capital costs because labour flows are not nearly as fluid and global as those of capital. Ergo, workers in one country have a somewhat greater ability to gain or maintain higher wages and benefits than banks and other financial institutions can charge higher interest rates than those in other countries. For instance, the differences in the yield that British and continental banks provide are minuscule compared to the differences in salaries and benefits. Given that general inflation rates reflect both labour and capital costs, and given that one component – capital – is lower than the average, it is a mathematical certainty that the other – labour – will be higher.

17. For discussion of this concept, see Leadbeater C and Christie I, 1999, *To Our Mutual Advantage*, Demos, London, as well as Leadbeater C, 1997, *Civic Spirit: The big idea for a new political era*, Demos, London. See also Etzioni A, 1995, *The Spirit of Community*, Fontana Press, London.

18. Referred to in Leadbeater, 1997, ibid.

19. See Leadbeater C and Martin S, 1998, *The Employee Mutual*, Demos, London.

20. Wuthnow R, 1994, *Sharing the Journey: Support groups and America's new quest for community*, The Free Press, New York, 71.

21. Bentley T, 1998, *Learning Beyond the Classroom: Education for a changing world*, Routledge, London; Jupp B, 1999, *Living Together: Community life on mixed-tenure estates*, Demos, London.

22. See description in Warpole K and Greenhalgh L, 1996, *Park Life*, Comedia and Demos, London.

23. For more discussion see Leadbeater C, 1996, *The Self-Policing Society*, Demos, London.

24. 'Punishment to Fit the Crime?', *Daily Telegraph*, 11 February 1998.

25. Luke and Neville, 1998 (note 15).

26. See, for instance, Sampson R, 1997, 'Neighborhoods and Violent Crime: A multilevel study of collective efficacy,' *Science*, no 277, 918-924.

27. For background discussions see Jupp, 1999 (note 21) ; Gray, 1996 (note 5); Hargreaves I and Christie I, 1998, *Tomorrow's Politics*, Demos, London; Leadbeater and Christie, 1999 (note 17); Kruger D, 1998, *Access Denied?*, Demos, London; Mulgan G et al, 1997, *The British Spring*, Demos, London.

28. To the extent that the Blair government is increasingly seen as a 'nanny state' that nags the public and tries to establish moral codes from above, a clarification of the government position on this issue seems to be called for.

29. The values enshrine in the laws of the state in turn may be assessed by drawing on still more encompassing laws, such as those of the EU and the UN. For more discussion see Etzioni, 1996 (note 6).

30. As the UK moves closer to having a written constitution, or as it adopts EU codes, the American malaise of litigiousness may become more common on these shores. At the same time it is not at all obvious that written constitutions are superior to basic laws, common law and strong democratic traditions.

31. Giddens, 1998 (note 6); Etzioni, 1995 (note 17).

32. While I generally agree with Anthony Giddens, we differ on this point. He writes, 'Government has a whole cluster of responsibilities for its citizens and others, including the protection of the vulnerable. Old-style democracy, however, was inclined to treat rights as unconditional claims. With expanding individualism should come an extension of individual obligations.... As an ethical principle, 'no rights without responsibilities' must apply not only to welfare recipients, but to everyone.' Giddens, 1998 (note 6), 65-66.

33. For more discussion, see Briscoe I, 1995, *In Whose Service: Making community service work for the unemployed*, Demos, London.

34. To keep this crucial point in mind, one may refer to 'voluntary moral culture' as distinct from the coercive one, found in Afghanistan and Iran in an extreme form and, in more moderate ways, in many non-free societies.

35. 'Inclusion refers in its broadest sense to citizenship, to the civil and political rights and obligations that all members of a society should have, not just formally, but as a reality of their lives.' Giddens, 1998 (note 6). As Philip Selznick put it, 'All persons have the same intrinsic worth.... Everyone who is a person is equally an object of moral concern.' This is the essence of justice.' Selznick adds that the most important threat to social justice is social subordination. Hence social power should be 'dispersed and balanced' but not wiped out. See Selznick P, *Social Justice: A communitarian perspective*, 63.

36. In the United States, the state of Oregon contributed to the dialogue on appropriate healthcare provisions. In its healthcare plan, the state ranked 688 medial procedures according to their costs and benefits; ultimately, it was decided that the first 568 services listed would be covered by the Oregon Medicaid programme ('OK Expected for Oregon Health Plan', *Houston Chronicle*, 18 March 1993). Whether or not this was the right cut-off point cannot be determined without a detailed examination of the plan. The case shows, however, that the discussion of what must be included can be made in specific terms rather than as an abstract moral principle.

37. Nathanson S, 1998, *Economic Justice*, Prentice Hall Academic, New York.

38. 'Do the Dome!', *Washington Post*, 7 May 2000.

39. The conditions under which 'trade offs' may occur is discussed at length in Etzioni A, 1999, *The Limits of Privacy*, Basic Books, New York. Briefly, a trade off should be considered only if there is a major social problem, for instance the rapid spread of HIV, if there are no effective treatments that do not entail trade offs, and if the intrusions proffered are as minimal as possible.

40. The problems that arise from the increased commercialisation of the media and the concentration of ownership deserve a separate treatment. Suffice it to say here that publicly owned and operated media should be cherished and support for it expanded, best by granting them large endowments.

41. Blair T, 1997, *New Britain*, Westview Press, Boulder, Colorado, 51.

42. For further discussion of 'science courts,' see Smith GP II, 1999, 'Judicial

Decision Making In the Age of Biotechnology', *Notre Dame Journal of Law, Ethics & Public Policy*, no 93. See also: Mazur A, 1993, 'The Science Court: Reminiscence and Retrospective', *Risk*, 4, 161.

43. These can be ameliorated to some extent by high levels of immigration, that would pose a host of challenges all by itself, by deepening the tensions raised by multiculturalism

44. One must, of course, stress that no stigma should be attached to families that cannot have children or see themselves as psychologically ill qualified to bring them up.

45. Wilkinson H, 1997, *The Proposal: Giving marriage back to the people*, Demos, London.

46. The latter provides couples with the opportunity to voluntarily bind themselves to higher level of commitment by agreeing to participate in pre-marital counseling, counseling while married if one spouse requests it, and delaying divorce for two years if one partner files for it, except in cases where a crime has been committed. See, for example, Etzioni A and Rubin P, 1997, *Opportuning Virtue: Lessons of the Louisiana Covenant Marriage Law, a communitarian report*, The Communitarian Network, Washington, DC. <http://www.gwu.edu/~ccps>.

47. Wilkinson H, 1995, 'No Turning Back,' in Mulgan G, ed, 1997, *Life After Politics: New thinking for the twenty-first century*, Fontana Press, London, 32-40.

48. In Britain, several privately run prisons include the first established in 1992, the Wolds remand centre in North Humberside, the Blankenhurst prison near Redditch, and the Parc prison near Bridgend.

49. This approach deserves some elaboration. People who are inclined to commit crimes are deterred by two factors that relate to one another as two variables in a mathematical formula: size of penalty (Pe) multiplied by the probability of being caught and punished (Pr) equals public safety. That is, a higher level of public safety can be achieved by increasing either variable. Given that Pr costs much less than Pe in human social and economic terms, increasing Pr is obviously preferable. Moreover, given that data show that increases in Pr are much more effective than in Pe, these facts alone provide a compelling reason for trying to increase Pr rather than Pe in the next years. Grogger J, 1991, 'Certainty vs. Severity of Punishment', *Economic Inquiry*, no 29, 297-309.

50. Hermerijck A and Visser J, 1999, 'The Dutch Model: an obvious candidate for the "third way"?', *The European Journal of Sociology*, vol 40, no 1, 103.

51. This is of course much less of an issue when unemployment is low. However, having community jobs as an integral part of the programme is important even if these jobs become a major factor only in other situations.

52. I draw here on Mulgan et al, 1997 (note 27), 19.

53. See the community recycling initiatives described in Murray R, 1999, *Creating Wealth from Waste*, Demos, London.

54. Although to withhold at the source for investment requires broad based international agreements, to retard the flight of capital.

55. To what extent the European Structural Fund covers this matter remains to be established.

56. Davis E, 1998, *Public Spending*, Penguin Books, London.

57. Personal communication with Steven Teles.

58. Some minimal use of traditional resources are involved, such as charges for connecting to the internet, but the costs for these are trivial.

59. Among the matters that may need more attention are the ways candidates get around expenditure limits by not reporting certain costs, underreporting expenses (such as travel expenses for the candidate and his family), and by stocking up on electioneering supplies well before the election. See Klein L, 1999, 'On the brink of reform: Political party funding in Britain,' *Case Western Reserve Journal of Law*, no 31, 1-46.

60. Dodd P, 1995, *The Battle Over Britain*, Demos, London.

61. Myers DG, 2000, *The American Paradox: Spiritual hunger in an age of plenty*, Yale University Press, New Haven, Connecticut.

62. For additional discussion, see Etzioni A, 1998, 'Voluntary Simplicity: Characterization, select psychological implications and societal consequences', *Journal of Economic Psychology*, no 19, 619-643